ARCTIC
VEHICLES

WRITTEN BY
Keriann Kenney

We use many different vehicles in the Arctic!

Some vehicles are for the winter. Some vehicles are for the summer. And some vehicles are used all year long.

When there is snow on the ground, many people drive snowmobiles. Snowmobiles can also drive on ice. They are used for daily travel, hunting, and fun!

Some people travel by dogsled in the winter. In the past, people used dogsled teams to travel long distances and to go hunting. Today, dogsledding is mostly done for fun.

People can use a qamutiik on the snow and ice. A qamutiik can be pulled by a snowmobile or dogs. It is used to carry people, food, and supplies.

In the summer, people can go out on the water. Many people use motorboats on the water. Motorboats can carry people and supplies. They are used for hunting, camping, and to enjoy nice weather.

In the spring, summer, and fall, people can ride bicycles. People in the North mostly ride bicycles for fun. Riding a bicycle is also a great way to get exercise.

13

In the spring, summer, and fall, many people drive ATVs. ATV stands for all-terrain vehicle. This means it can go over many types of land. People drive ATVs to run errands, to travel to cabins, and to go hunting.

All year long, cars and trucks are used in communities in the North. They can carry more than one person and lots of supplies around a community.

All year long, people fly in planes. There are no roads connecting communities in the North. People use planes to travel to other communities or to the South. Planes are also used to carry supplies to other communities.

In the Arctic, we use a lot of different vehicles to travel around our communities and on the land.